365 Principles
of
Success

In quotations and anecdotes

EUGINE MAKAYA

ISBN:-10: 1-5302-0316-3
ISBN-13: 978-1-5302-0316-1

DEDICATION

This book is dedicated to Shanell Christian Nashe.

_____Your success heritage _____

CONTENTS

EUGINE MAKAYA

ACKNOWLEDGMENTS

All reviewers of this book are acknowledged for their contributions.

INTRODUCTION

Mankind is always desperately looking for solutions to a multitude of daily challenges. However, the rate of success is deplorable. So should people not keep on exploring opportunities for success? No. The level of desperation is tantamount to spending the whole day fishing from a bathtub using live and scented rubber worms, spinning hooks and classic Rapala rods. The approach may sound intelligible but the logic is questionable. Therefore, the recipe to success is in transforming one's mental constructs into reality.

365 Principles of Success is an outline of success principles in the form of quotations and anecdotes. It attempts to stir and awaken the sleeping giant in you. Remember giants are not giants in their sleep; some

even woke up being chased by ants.

This book is only a guide. To get the best out of it, take one quotation each day, meditate upon it, create a suitable home or business situation, apply the principle and visualize yourself in a state of success. For 365 days reading this book, you will never remain the same.

Good reading!

A

AGE

 Poverty stinks worse than an over-age he-goat.

 As wrinkles are signs of age, so is wealth a sign of success. Both cannot be hidden.

ALWAYS

 Teach a pig a new trick, the result will always be the same.

 Well-wishers always feel well.

B

BEHIND

✶ Never be intimidated by followers, they always follow from behind.

✶ Driving is not an easy task. You concentrate on those behind you, those within you and those ahead of you.

BETTER

✶ A flowing river is better than a dead pond.

✶ Orderly disorder is better than no order at all.

✶ Better be flexible than rigid. Flexibility takes you far.

ℵ An oat-meal consumed is better than a planned buffet.

BEYOND

ℵ Your eyes cannot see beyond where you can hear.

ℵ If your surroundings can't influence you, look beyond the horizon.

ℵ If you cannot read between lines, read beyond lines.

BREAK

ℵ A broken springboard breaks the spine.

ℵ Pretence is very dangerous. One day hell will break loose.

BUSINESS

ℵ The business of the mind is the business.

ℵ In science energy is the ability to do work, but in business it is the ability to make profits.

ℵ I don't see a joke in success. It's a serious business.

C

CERTAIN

א   Certain ideas can be hidden under a carpet but not under tile.

א   However dark it may be tonight, tomorrow, day is certain.

CHANGE

א   Money is a means of exchange; you pay the bearer on demand.

א   The only bad thing about change is that it makes you leave your old ways.

א   When suffering becomes unbearable change is inevitable.

- Remaining unchanged in a changing world is defying the cause of nature.

- Those who stand in the way of change are changed by it.

- The volume of a balloon does not change by inflation.

COMPETITION

- Competition is for the competitive; the fearful have no part to play.

- A competition is not a competition until your competitors give up.

COURAGE

- For the courageous, retreating is going forward in the negative direction.

- Courage is not in the talk but the walk.

- Courage is the strength but confidence is the impetus.

- Principles are the guidelines. Courage is the means.

- A man of courage has courage to seek counsel.

D

DECEPTION

- ℵ Cheating is all about self-deception; those that indulge cheat themselves.

- ℵ Deception has no experienced, even fish are caught by rubber worms.

DECISION

- ℵ Decision making is a process while a decision is eventful.

- ℵ Success is not a decision by others but comes from others for others.

- ℵ Varying opinions are fundamentals of successful decisions.

א In a meeting, the chair is the least. He decides on others' decisions.

DETERMINE

א Success determinants are not determined by drama.

א It is the detergent that can determine the dirty on your clothes.

א It can be late now, but it's not too late. Success is not determined by dawn or dusk.

א Obstacles on your way determine your speed.

DIFFERENCE

א The difference between white and black is in the pigmentation.

א The difference between men is the success of this world.

א The difference between materials is the raw material.

א The difference between a buying decision and a decision to succeed is in the legal tender.

א The difference between new and old clothes is in their exposure to water.

DILIGENCE

- ℵ The success of a diligent man brings trouble to his adversaries. Fear not!

- ℵ Train a child in diligence and a nation is established.

DOOR

- ℵ Keys are unique they don't open on every door.

- ℵ An open door is the same when closed.

DREAM

- ℵ Dreams unrealised are successes buried.

- ℵ When big dreamers dream, their dreams are too small.

- ℵ A dream unrealised is a delusion.

- ℵ No two people are the same. The difference is in their dreams.

- ℵ Success is not success until it is shared; otherwise it's only a dream. Dreams cannot be shared.

- ℵ Choice is not a dream; you can make it in broad daylight.

- ℵ When people start dreaming of your success then you are successful.

א A desire is nothing else but a premature dream.

E

EDUCATION

א Education is good. It closes open doors.

א Brains and education are a means and an end.

א Education is the character in it.

EXPERIENCE

א Your ability to realise your inexperience is good experience for success.

א Experience teaches an experienced mind.

F

FAILURE

א Success is a birth right while failure is a self-made heritage.

א For the greedy, failure is their daily bread.

א Poor minds fantasise on the failure of others.

א Failure to forgive is doubling your hurt.

א Failure is believing that what has not been done cannot be done.

FAITH

א Beyond the furthest distance eyes can see faith goes.

א The faith of a parachutist is in the air.

FAST

א A prickly way causes those that walk on it to walk faster.

ℵ A tortoise can run faster than a cheetah, only in a movie.

ℵ Only fast followers get followed.

FEAR

ℵ Don't masquerade to be fearless; those excuses are a manifestation of fear.

ℵ The fearful are the slaves of the fearless.

ℵ Once feared, twice erred.

ℵ People succeed by succeeding to conquer their fears.

ℵ Fear and mediocrity are doomed cousins.

FIGHT

ℵ The difference between two fighting men is virtue.

ℵ Only the wise people fight to become better friends tomorrow.

ℵ Fight a successful man, he will be more successful.

ℵ Fighters are deaf, they only hear after the fight.

FINISH

ℵ Sprinters never bother where they tread, but where they finish.

א   Learning is like cooking where ingredients are transformed into the finished product.

א   When you run and fall, rise up and go, you never know the one ahead of you might faint before getting to the finishing line.

FIRE

א   Test gold by fire and you won't regret the result.

א   If your employer takes too long to fire you, then fire yourself.

FOCUS

א   The danger of focusing on top positions is that it blinds you from seeing the way to the top.

א   Foresight is focus.

א   In a roundtable meeting, the focus is not on the round table.

FOLLOW

א   The world is always turning around and those that follow it turn around.

א   Having followed all principles for success. The next step is divine.

※ Instincts should be followed as should be divine intervention.

FOOL

※ Enlightenment develops all negatives, while foolishness negates all developments.

※ Chiding a fool is fuelling his fury.

※ Wisdom appends understanding while foolishness depends on vanity.

FRIENDSHIP

※ A successful person does not know all his friends.

※ A good name bears countless friends.

※ Bad friends are like rotten potatoes; they spoil each other.

※ Poverty is an enemy. Those that befriend it always regret.

G

GOOD

א Pretending to be sick is good proof of your sickness.

א A good song is not in the lyrics but where it takes you.

א Enemies are good; they help the successful remain afloat.

א Good plans are not a result of over-planning. They are fit for a purpose.

א Gravity is good. It pulls down the proud.

א Tension is good, but hypertension leads to stroking.

א The good thing about mental highways is that there are no traffic jams.

א Success is a good beginning and a good ending.

H

HEART

- אּ If your heart cannot see where you are going better not go.
- אּ Level headed people have their hearts outside.

HUMILITY

- אּ Submission is humility for a mission.
- אּ Business etiquette is a game of humility.

I

IDEA

- אּ Homes manufacture ideas but offices refine them.
- אּ The logic of an idea is in its accomplishments.

א Don't run after other people's ideas. When you get them, there will be new ones.

א The number of times an idea fails in your mind is the same number it will fail in reality.

א The idea of a good idea is in an idea.

א When you give up on an idea. It is a good idea to share it.

א An innovation is a better idea of an idea.

IMAGINATION

א Imagination is the epicentre of all inventions.

א The most abundant resource in this world is imagination; with it you can create a new world.

INNOVATION

א Innovation is the ability to make existing things obsolete.

א The test of innovation is in the taste of success.

א I wonder why people don't innovate. Because they live by innovation.

א Discoverers see what has not been seen while innovators differently see what has been seen.

N Innovation is drawing correct solutions from wrong premises.

N When people run out of innovation, they imitate each other.

N Lack of innovation makes an organisation dead alive.

N Innovators are like gynaecologists, they bring out new life.

N Why wait for redundancy. Innovate now!

INTEGRITY

N Integrity defines success while corruption defines failure.

N Integrity is more integrating that deceit.

N Question the integrity of a leader and tomorrow you will lead.

N When tempers flare, integrity takes you down.

J

JOURNEY

- ℵ Take a journey and excuse those who don't know its purpose.

- ℵ Going on a journey, be careful who holds your stuff.

- ℵ End your journey by starting a new one.

- ℵ It is only him who has started a journey who can be delayed.

K

KNOWLEDGE

- ℵ A novice knows no novel.

- ℵ To venture or not to venture. Know where you stand. You cannot be in between.

- א The deaf and the dumb are no different. They both don't know one world.

- א Givers are never broke; they know where to get the gifts.

- א Toymakers design toys knowing that there are young adults.

- א An experiment with known results is not worth carrying out.

- א Ignorance is never a problem. It is temporary. New knowledge acquired leaves re-markable trails.

- א Knowledge is mystical; you need enough for the day.

L

LEADERSHIP

- א Success is leadership applied.

- א Leadership is not in the top management. It is in the middle management elevated to the top.

א   A leader whose leadership is not replicated is only a replica.

א   Respect of opinions is an attribute of successful leadership. How many opinions have you respected?

א   Leadership is like salt, it seasons the seasoned.

א   Follow the leader to be a followed leader.

א   A leader who does not see the position of his subordinates is in a wrong position.

א   Leaders are blind to themselves. All they see are opportunities.

א   Leaders are underwriters. Their organisations require no further assurance.

א   Insecure leaders are gatekeepers, nothing new comes their way.

א   The most detrimental thing you can do as a leader is to walk with your brains above your hat.

א   Walking up a staircase, you don't become a leader when you are on the last step.

א   A daring leader is a caring leader.

א   A leader without a following is just a follower.

א   A leader who leads by intimidation is a leader without a leader.

LIES

א   Lies are quick to set in human minds. Were it possible, they would have been used for dam construction.

א   What lies in you is greater than what lies in fallen heroes.

LIFE

א   To walk on water, put on a life jacket.

א   Astronomers believe all life came from early stars. So you are star material.

M

MAKE

א   A triangle is three sided. The absence of one makes it a bi-angle.

א   Make a shovel a spade and it will be.

MAN

א   Love is so blind that even a blind man can see it.

א   One man's mountain is another man's hump.

א   A decision by one man, still needs to be decided on.

א   A man of many words is choked by his own.

MANY

א   Trivials are by one, but committees are by many.

א   Better a planted seed than many in a granary.

א   The inventor of a ballpoint pen knew many would use it.

א   There are many opportunities in laziness of mankind. One of them is the invention of remote controls.

א   Success manifests itself in many ways. One of it is a new world.

א   There are many schools of thought. One of them is in you.

MEANING

א   There is more meaning in a conclusion than the rest of the story.

- ℵ When people don't venture their adventures are without meaning.

MEMORY

- ℵ Human memory is limited. That's why there are recipe books.
- ℵ Memory is the archive, comprehension comes by it.
- ℵ Repeat yourself to be understood because human memory is as fast as lightning.

MIND

- ℵ With electricity you can boil water, but with the mind you can stir the world.
- ℵ Provoked minds are like arrows in a quiver. If unleashed they wreak havoc.
- ℵ The will and the mind are the only Faculty of the Future.
- ℵ Resilience is only a causal relationship between the mind and success goals.
- ℵ The mind is a key to open mindful doors.
- ℵ If you put down your mind, the next generation will pick it up.
- ℵ A man is not in his voice but in his mind.

℘   An idle mind will always be idling.

℘   Only a sound mind can quench a bubbling tongue.

MISTAKES

℘   Only mistakes take centre stage in a blame game.

℘   Learning from mistakes is success assumed.

℘   Original mistakes are the origins of many successes.

N

NEVER

℘   If your employer has never worked for you, why continue working?

℘   Note that a rear view mirror is never in the rear. Thus, being led does not mean you cannot lead.

℘   Ship builders never forget furious storms.

NOT

℘   Varying opinions from a subordinate do not imply insubordination.

- Greed does not breed.

- If things are not moving, why waiting for them?

- It is water that quenches the thirst and not the thirst that quenches water.

- A microscope magnifies small objects, but not itself.

NOTHING

- Choose a profession that interests you and get paid for doing nothing.

- The purpose of a knife is to cut, nothing else.

- Watch mushrooms grow and you will see nothing.

NUMBER

- Respect is number one ingredient in a success bakery.

- It's not in the number of quotations you read but in your success quotation.

O

ONLY

א Only high fliers can stoop to conquer.

א Cooking is not the only way of making food palatable.

א It's only a fallacy to sow thorns and reap corn.

א It is only a scissors that cuts in one direction.

א Only the indomitable can dominate their environment inexorably.

א It is only a coward who speaks through silence.

א It is only the density test that can tell if milk has been diluted with water.

א If I can't be a multi-millionaire, then I can only be a billionaire.

א It takes only the modest to take a bull by its horns.

א Only early birds are haste and swift, they always catch the best.

א Only when you pay for friendship, you pay for your downfall.

OPPORTUNITY

✶   When you miss an opportunity hunt after others.

✶   A missed opportunity is not a lost opportunity.

✶   Never rest on your laurels, your best today may be the worst tomorrow.

✶   Waiting for an opportunity is like waiting for the rains in winter.

✶   Hurry is where it is accorded an opportunity.

✶   Success is not in a higher degree but in untapped opportunities.

ORGANISE

✶   When a disorganised person organises, his organisation agonises.

✶   The only risk in any organisation is managing risk management.

✶   In the absence of organisational culture, cultures develop.

✶   Without the head organisations should function. Even a cockroach lives long without it.

OTHERWISE

א   Refuse to be given always, otherwise you become a beggar.

א   Be careful of caregivers, otherwise they will take care of you.

א   Holidays are for the industrious, otherwise you are on holiday.

P

PEOPLE

א   When two people disagree, each one of them agrees to his own opinion.

א   Outstanding discoveries are not by outstanding people. You can discover yourself.

א   People are not happy because of any excitement but because they choose to.

POWER

א   A pen is more powerful than a bow and an arrow.

א   The power of a machine gun is in the trigger.

PROMOTE

א   If the promotion does not come, then promote yourself.

א   Don't be disappointed when you are not promoted. There is no one who can do your job better.

R

RACE

א   Results of an unfinished race are no different from results of a race not started.

א   The reward of outcompeting others in a race is the price.

א   Run a race with a true leader. He will lead.

א   Never run a race when you don't know the finishing point. You may end up where you started.

RICH AND POOR

ℵ   The main difference between riches and wealth is in the mind of the wealthy.

ℵ   The difference between the rich and the poor is in the amounts they spend.

ℵ   Only the poor in mind, mind pointing fingers at others.

ℵ   Take advantage of the poor and your success will be vanity.

S

SENSE

ℵ   Common sense is common; with it you know who you are.

ℵ   Trying is not a problem as long as there is tried sense.

SIZE

﹅ You have your own size, why going for one-size-fits-all?

﹅ The success of a runner is not in the size of his strides.

﹅ It's not in the thunder that determines the size of a bolt.

SLEEP

﹅ Envy not when the successful rise up early and sleep late. That's where their success comes from.

﹅ Let sleeping dogs lie because in their sleep they expend their energy.

﹅ A prisoner is only free when he is asleep.

STRENGTH

﹅ In a game of chess, the strength of the King is in the pawn.

﹅ Only fish can gauge the strength of a current.

﹅ It is the strength in an acid that makes it useful in batteries. Otherwise water could have been an alternative.

א The strength of steel is different from that of wood. The difference is in the process of formation.

א The strength of a weak man is in the strength of other man.

א Only an ant can tell you the strength of an elephant.

א Strong arguments are not in the number of words, as sound minds are portals of wisdom.

א The human mind is much stronger than the deadliest weapon ever invented. With it you can blow mountains.

א Failure is a strong code of moral decadence. To break it succeed!

א Challenges are for the strong while excuses are for the feeble.

SUCCESS

א Success is a culture whose initiation starts with the mind.

א Success battles are not won by machine guns but by mental war-cries.

- ℵ Self-understanding is the first module in a success course.

- ℵ Success is a noun and a verb.

- ℵ Success is only success when defined by the successful.

- ℵ As food is for nourishment, so is successful reading for success.

- ℵ Be mindful about what you sign for. You may be signing for the success of somebody.

- ℵ Success is not where you are going but where you should be going.

- ℵ There is nothing new under the sun; the only new thing is your success.

- ℵ Success in silence makes the greatest noise.

- ℵ Never mind discouragement, it will still be there after your success.

- ℵ Like body and soul, longevity and success are inseparable.

- ℵ Success is like a diamond. It is a product of heat and pressure.

- ℵ Success is sweet. I am surprised by those who can't discern it.

- ℵ When did you last talk about success? To yourself!

ℵ   Self-centeredness centrifuges success.

ℵ   Success is not impulsive, a process leads to it.

ℵ   Success starts at its endpoint.

ℵ   Advertisers surprise me. Imagine appending a picture of a half-naked person to a model car. With such wit they succeed.

ℵ   Limitations are ubiquitous. There will be even more limitations when you succeed.

T

TIME

ℵ   A man of too many words falls too many times.

ℵ   Time is a continuous variable. Never say I will do it in the next hour.

ℵ   The value of time is in the time success is sustained.

ℵ   Run behind time and your time will be behind.

ℵ   What time is it now? It is time to time your goals.

ℵ   To succeed in a race of time is to be ahead of time.

- ℵ Time is limited, that's why the old wish they were young.

- ℵ Don't be caught up with technology fever, where people spend most of their time learning the technology instead of using it.

- ℵ Don't put all your eggs in one basket; otherwise they will hatch at the same time.

- ℵ A stich in time saves nine, while nine stitches in time save hundred.

- ℵ You can only be right to the right people at the right time.

- ℵ Ice is not volatile it melts by its time.

- ℵ Time is just but an indicator.

THOSE

- ℵ Those that go after money come second.

- ℵ Hearsay is unbelievable. Those that say it, say it in private.

- ℵ Those suffering from wait-and-see syndrome really see in their waiting as others prosper.

- ℵ Poverty is brutal and ruthless. Those that are caught up with it are devastated.

- ℵ Those that labour in vain, labour for their masters.

TRUST

א Put not your trust in a man who does not trust in himself.

א A man with dirty hands deserves no entrustment.

א Trust humble beginnings because they are humble.

TRUTH

א A lawyer does not change the truth but deciphers the facts.

א A false statement is like a burning forest, only truth can quench it.

א Truth needs no supporting words. It's true.

א Truth is not defined by multitudes.

V

VALUE

א What you pay for innovation is the value of the innovation.

The value of life is not in the time used, but time wasted.

 The value of a signature is in the worthy of the contract.

VISION

 Your vision is not easily seen by your peers. They need vision to see your vision.

 If you cannot see what has not been seen then you don't have a vision.

 Visions are contagious. Be careful whose vision you contract.

 It takes vision to see light at the end of the tunnel. Only vision can take you there.

W

WEAK

 For the weak, it is a mountain to climb a mountain.

א The weakness of a one-man band is the absence of backing vocals.

א Don't hide your weaknesses; they may be someone's source of success.

WHY AND WHERE

א The sun rises from the East and sets in the West. Where?

א Why have bicycles gained more popularity than tricycles?

א Why are metals galvanised? It is because there is rust all over.

WIN

א Character wins all your battles, whether in the valley or on the mountains.

א In a race, the success of a winner is in the failure of others competitors.

א When one man runs a race, there are no winners.

WIND

א When wind blows, to know its direction face it.

א   Winds of change always blow; it takes imagination to discern the direction.

א   When wind blows, blow with it.

WISDOM

א   Wisdom is the accumulation of knowledge while accumulation of wisdom is maturity.

א   A positive change in wisdom is success

א   Shoes are for the feet but wisdom is for success.

א   It takes all into the ears, but out of the mind wisdom.

א   The mind is just like a bank, the only accepted legal tender is wisdom.

א   Users of transparent packaging want you to appreciate the contents.

א   Wisdom is materialistic. It is yet another state of matter.

א   Dine with the wise to dine their wisdom.

WRONG

א   A wrong equation will always give wrong answers.

א   The wrong thing about individualism is lack of rationalism.

א   A wrongly encoded message jams the decoder.

Y

YOU

א   Sharpen your axe before you fell a tree.

א   First disposition yourself to position yourself for greatness.

א   First be influenced in order for you to influence.

א   If a mosquito can fly and an aeroplane can fly, why can't you?

א   Take the ungrateful half way, they ask you to go all the way.

א   That non-supportive background is the right springboard to elevate you beyond your peers.

M

MISCELLANEOUS

א   The best way to eat a pomegranate is by squeezing out the juice.

א   Pain from exercise is sweet but pain from idleness is bitter.

א   Empty vessels are always full of void.

א   Preparation is an art while execution is a science.

א   Sight without perception is sight-seeing.

א   The advantage of a psychological boundary is that it can be crossed easily.

א   Contentment is containment, from it comes no new thing.

א   Even woodworms are selective; they don't bore all types of wood.

א   Motivation simply means motive and action combined.

א   Fishermen are very patient. Even if they don't catch, they wait until the fish are hungry.

א   Giving up is a game of the given up.

ℵ   Fuel of a car is at the rear, but it works in front.

ℵ   A damp-proof course proofs by damping.

ℵ   Building a legacy starts by building credibility.

ℵ   A picture is really a false image of reality.

ℵ   To measure body temperature use a thermometer, for temperament use discretion.

ℵ   A duplicate is a duplicate. It will never match the original.

CONCLUSION

Therefore, success is not for any special people. It comes to all and for all who desire and purpose to succeed. Success has no bounds or limits.

However you have understood this book, success remains an unchallenged truth. Take a giant step towards your life dreams. Today is the day and there is no other better day to start actualizing your dreams. You don't need any further inspiration.

Draw a plan, with time frames, to guide you through your success journey. Do not limit yourself by giving excuses for not starting today. Remember procrastination is a thief of time. You have everything that you need to start this journey.

The whole world is waiting to be changed by you. Your success is a worldly success.

ABOUT THE AUTHOR

Eugine Makaya is an acclaimed author of numerous bestselling books. He is an academic, educator and author. Eugine has written books in Engineering, Science and Management. He is also a cofounder of the Sustainable Development Institute. He can be contacted at eugine.makaya@gmail.com